ID'S HOSPIT

To my parents

Sheenagh Pugh
ID'S HOSPIT

seren

seren
is the book imprint of
Poetry Wales Press Ltd
First Floor, 2 Wyndham Street
Bridgend, Wales

Cataloguing In Publication Data for this title
is available from the British Library

ISBN 1-85411-177-9

The publisher works with the financial support of the
Arts Council of Wales

Cover: from an original photograph by Michael Burns
of the former St David's Hospital in Canton, Cardiff

Printed in Palatino by
The Cromwell Press, Melksham

Contents

What If This Road

What if this road, that has held no surprises
these many years, decided not to go
home after all; what if it could turn
left or right with no more ado
than a kite-tail? What if its tarry skin
were like a long, supple bolt of cloth,
that is shaken and rolled out, and takes
a new shape from the contours beneath?
And if it chose to lay itself down
in a new way; around a blind corner,
across hills you must climb without knowing
what's on the other side; who would not hanker
to be going, at all risks? Who wants to know
a story's end, or where a road will go?

Sailing to Islands

There is always a time, sailing to islands,
when you notice they have turned green,
and they weren't, when you set out. They began blue,
a blur of deeper blue at the sky's edge,

hardly a smudge, an ache in the straining eye,
but they are hardening now into solid ground,
a green presence, and the sea goes on
beyond them; they are not the end after all.

Already the land is dividing into fields:
soon you will see houses, roads, a harbour.
Look back: it is the port where you embarked
that is nowhere now, lost in a blue shadow.

There must have been a moment when past and future
changed colour; when your journey was suddenly nearer
its end than its beginning. Your mind wandered
on porpoises, or fulmars, or a cloud

fretted with light, and the moment slipped by;
it always does. There is nothing unknown,
any more, about where you are going,
that distant landfall; it is all laid out

before you, so much more real now
than the blue mainland of memory.
The sea goes on further, but not for you;
there is no escaping the safe harbour.

Like the Keen of Hamar

A man could be hard and silver
like the Keen of Hamar;
an ice-age, a stony moon outcrop
of serpentine debris.
Yet every crack of his selfhood
would shine with rarities. The white stars
of northern rock cress, of sandwort,
of mountain everlasting, would make
a sanctuary of him.

Or he might be as anchorless
as the sands of Sumburgh,
yet even in such drifting shallows,
sea-rocket would root. Each year,
faint-scented succulents would claw back
more beach; where was once
a wandering shelf of bareness,
folk would pick their way
through the green tangles.

And though he could stand as sheer
as the red sandstone crag
that is the Noup of Noss,
yet wind and sea would scratch crevices
in his side to shelter the white
shapeless fluff of fulmar chicks,
and the lichen of love would come about him;
a thousand gannetries would steep each bluff
in the acrid tang of belonging.

Sandman

Cloud has scrolled over again, and a cold wind
blows seals into the bay; black brows gleaming
on a gunmetal sea, and there is no-one left
on the beach except me and the naked man,

lying face down in the sand. He is growing paler
as he dries out: small silent grains are sliding
down the slopes of him, filling the hollow
of his back. Four sets of footprints lead away

from the body: his and his wife's, going straight ahead,
and a circling turmoil from the boy and girl,
too old for sandcastles, who took so much trouble
sculpting their murder victim. They were laughing

all the time, and the patient father, stretched out
on the beach to be posed and measured, was laughing too,
shaking his head, complaining his sepia likeness
was too short, building up muscles of sand....

His wife sat watching the dead man take shape
under her children's hands. She kept trailing
her fingers through her hair; as it fell back,
the grey would catch the light. She never laughed

with the others: even the brief smile flitting
across her face went out whenever she glanced
from her husband to the body like his.
When the sky darkened, and they were going,

she wanted to know if the tide would take him.
And they said no: he was above the mark,
and she left, reassured. I watched her out of sight
an hour since, and already his right hand has blurred

into a white hummock. Wind shivers over him,
evening him out: soon the little sand-crabs,
scribbling their hasty messages on silence,
won't even have to pause when they come on him.

Brief Lives

Papa Stour

An island huddles against the gale
like a hunched shoulder. Fleece, manes, hair,
grass, tears: all streaming.

Trudging against it, eyes down,
fixed on the ground. It's moving;
flakes of ash scudding seawards

then, suddenly, lifted
on a gust, tossed high. They're moths,
hundreds, pale see-through scraps

of airmail. They can't cling
to grass or stone; everything loose is leaving.
They can't steer;

can't assert themselves on a sky
that's pure movement. The wind is full
of waste paper;

brief wordless messages
fluttering out unread
over the Atlantic.

Under Way

As the ferry got under way, he looked out
from its stern, filling his eyes with the wall
by the quayside, where he and Cal and Lowrie
killed so much time; and the island's one poky shop,
full of dead sell-by dates; and saithe pegged out
on a clothes-line drying; and Anderson's cat
taking a stroll. As they cleared the mouth
of the harbour, someone waved from the hill,
and it might have been Cal, but he couldn't see
for sure, and he fixed his gaze on one window
in one of the whitewashed houses. The boat lifted
on a strong swell; plunged; flew again,
with the spray stinging. A couple of tourists,
wide-eyed, were watching the gannets dive
on fish, as if it were something special,
and already the roads were gone; the island became
two low green hills with a gleam of white
in the dip, where the houses were, just at the end
of the boat's wake. The mainland was edging nearer
behind a haze, sunlight drizzled through cloud,
but the island's micro-climate shone
under a bell-jar of blue glassy sky.
Sometimes it nearly vanished in a band of light
on the horizon, but if he screwed his eyes,
crusted with salt, he could still make a shape out,
and though the scattering wake no longer reached
so far, he could follow the line back
to the white gleam: it was still there, but only
because he knew it was.

The Old Road

Most of the old road is buried under
the new. Just now and then, the grey track
slips alongside: asphalt going back
to grass, disappearing in the heather.
It led to town; it took every crofter
thrown off the land. Young lads, out to make
a fortune, turned away from home to take
the narrow road that led to something better,
to steady work, money put by,
or the graveyard cough and a parish funeral.
Sometimes you can fancy a file of shadows
tramping this road: wary, stoical,
dreaming ahead, keeping their hopes high,
their thin coats open to every wind that blows.

Didn't They Shine

Quendale, 1992

I didn't see any seals that day,
but then I wasn't looking. It was enough
to lie in a white dune, watching the wind
make patterns. The way the sand shifted,
glinting in the light. The grey fur
of rabbits; the silver snail-trails
in the air.

                It wasn't the Atlantic
in my ears, nor planes, nor birds. I was wired up
to a man singing a song of old love.
"Didn't we shine", he purred, while the length
of bright beach dissolved in the sun,
and the waves shattered, perfect whiteness
detonating rainbows. "It wasn't meant
to last till the end of time."

And I lay back, thinking it would,
and closed my eyes, as if I had years left
to look. I can still recall
the wave-crests, the grains like powdered quartz
through my fingers: didn't they shine, didn't they.

Voices in Mousa Broch

Part I

1994

No-one lives on this island any more,
but all summer, all day when the ferry runs,
the tower is filled with languages: sibilant
Japanese whispers in the double walls;
Dutch gutturals echoing on the stone steps,
French, Danish, nasal New York; they come to exclaim
into the steep height; admire its craftsmanship.

By nightfall they are scattered abroad again,
and the wall, that shammed so dumb all day,
comes alive, chattering, purring, hiccupping,
in a reeking patter of storm petrels;
its night-speech, its true summer language,
whose memory lasts it through the censorship
of snow, and the long monologue of wind.

Part II

To Earl Harald in Orkney, greeting.
There has been no change. We are still outside
Mousa Broch, where we have been sitting
some weeks. In your last message, you suggested

we take it by storm. Have you ever seen
the place? It is a stone tower, quite round,
with walls a yard thick, and one way in.
From its top, look-outs scan the whole island,

which boasts not a bush nor a tree for cover,
and God knows we could do with some, to dodge
the constant showers of arrows coming over.
They are well equipped, if I am any judge,

and well manned. The siege goes on, hampered
by the fact that we can find little to eat
in this bare place. The broch is stuffed with food;
he had it all planned out, I must admit.

We hear your mother singing, quite often:
she once climbed to the rampart, which we thought
remarkable at her age. The young man,
her lover, was there too, and in shot,

but they held hands, and we dared not chance
hitting her. She laughs a lot, these days,
and looks better. She shouted to me once
from the wall: "Tell my son I love this place".

If you were to ask me, I should say
that she was old enough to know her mind;
that I miss my bed; that my farm in Orkney
must be going to the dogs, and that this Erlend

of hers is one damn clever soldier
who would make a useful ally. The chill rain
has soaked into my bones, I shouldn't wonder:
I never want to see this place again.

Part III

circa 909

I can't take my eyes off the fire:
I'm fixed here, staring into the flames,
listening for their soft flap, and the sputter
when someone feeds them. They wrap themselves
round the dark. Eyes scorching, I can forget
Thorir Hroaldsson on the high seas
seeking my life.

Arnor is checking what stores were saved
from the wreck; seeing them stacked
in the rooms — rooms! Scrapes in the wall,
shadows seeping from the thick stone.
The girl in my arm shivers against me:
"They look like troll-holes".

Her mouth tastes cold and sweet.
Because of her, I am hunted.
I stroke her hair, thinking: *I could die
for this*, and the blonde strands crackle
and burn my hand.

Arnor has posted sentries
on the wall's top, distant as stars.
He grins at me: "The little folk built
to keep out raiders. Odd, really:
would you think the poor bloody goblins
had anything worth taking?"

She burrows under my cloak,
her numbed fingers nuzzling
inside my shirt; my skin jumps.
Staring beyond the flames,
I see our shadows shift
on the wall: two dark folk
seeking shelter, like us and not like.

Part IV

?

When you stoop in our doorways
you will feel we were small.
Measure our fear
by the wall's thickness.

The gulls that nest
each year where we lived
leave no less behind.
Our stone benches
took no impress.

In the shadows
of low-roofed cells
you guess at us;
around the bends
of narrow stairways.

But all you know
is the hollow in the millstone,
and a white midden
of empty sea-shells.

The Fiddler Willie Hunter

1933-1994

An old man is playing the fiddle, perfectly,
slow as pouring honey, all his days
distilled into the notes. This is his tune,
a glass filling with light and white water,
and sons a world away, and ships sailing,
and every fiddler on this windy island,
alive or long dead, who ever made
a lament, and named it for a friend.

He has been dead a month, this old man
who lives in the VCR; whose great gift
can be turned on when I choose to hear
his music. All that learning: all that grief
and joy turned off, as if the perfection
of a life's art were such a little thing
to the indifferent finger on the switch
that flicked him into darkness without thinking.

In his last weeks, racked with the sureness
of death coming, he spent day after day
in a basement room, laying down his music
on tape. He played without food, without rest,
till pain exhausted him; he would sit a moment,
then play again. They say he was never
so fired up; never put such loss
and passion into "Leaving Lerwick Harbour".

Last week a boy of fourteen, his pupil,
took first prize, playing the old man's air
to the best judges, but behind his eyes
he was playing to his master.... And there will always
be such another, and the strings will always ring,
and a man be remembered in love
who has left a tune, or bent a boy's fingers
to the bow, though it is not enough,

nor the face on the screen that cannot be moved
any more by love; nor the twenty tunes he left,
nor the young pupils. There are still the other tunes
his mind never shaped, and all the pupils
who never knew him. Those he lived among
will keep him, because they were not done with him,
and would never have flicked the black switch,
being more generous than gods, or death, or time.

This Basement Room

This basement room. No sun gets in.
Its walls are soundproof. Outside,
the air reeks of fish; a raucous scrum
of gulls goes down on the harbour scraps,
and your wife's shoes clatter on the flags
as she hums your tunes. You wouldn't know.

The light slips by: six hours a day
in the northern winter. July nights
will be blue, uncertain; sun dawdling
on the sea's rim, no-one going to bed,
but you know you'll be dead by summer.
This basement room: hour after hour

you make music. The blank tapes fill with tunes,
tunes that waited, these many years,
while you ran the laundry, drove taxis,
fed your family. You're no Gauguin;
you were too good a man to be free.
The light slips by, but what is left,

all your life, now, belongs to you
and your fiddle, and its loosed voice.
One bright morning, you felt guilty:
asked your wife if she'd like to go out,
spend time with you, and she answered:
"You make music: I'll bring food."

Your death coming set you free.
For all the pain, your bow-arm
flexes easy as ebb-tide
over the notes; easy as a man
coming home after years away.
All your life you wanted this:

this basement room. The waiting tunes
belong to you, and all your life
fills the blank tapes. She brings you food
and sets you free. For all the pain,
she hums your tunes. The light slips by.
Your death coming, you make music.

The Time is Now

Never saw a sky so blue,
so keen a light, all summer long.
The time is now:
this month, this week, to walk among
the burning trees, till they snuff out.

In the great park there stands an elm,
yellower than sun in its chain-mail
of shivering flame.
The choir-school boys are playing ball,
team-kitted, shrill-voiced, making fun

behind Sir's back, or watching where
a girl swings past. The note of red
rings in her hair;
in rowan leaves; in the splashed blood
of berries; in the smouldering west.

The gates will shut before too long.
Late in the day; late in the year.
They look so young,
the girl with her bright fall of hair,
the boys in yellow, like the tree.

Two Retired Spymasters

They settled down beside the Suffolk coast,
in the flat lands where men can see for miles
— no hills to hide behind; no tricky forest —
They liked the villagers' polite, closed smiles,

the way a stranger always stayed a stranger.
They used to practise merging with the crowd
of tourists at the festival each summer,
just out of habit; just to show they could.

In the Cross Keys, trying to reminisce
without infringing Acts of Parliament,
they'd talk in hints, pauses, half-sentences.
And sometimes, by the window, they fell silent,

gazing out at the dark, the sundown sea,
and the tired, sunken faces in the glass,
thinking how surely the last enemy
was edging up, for all their watchfulness.

Undercover

She walked toward me in a wall of glass,
so well disguised.
I swear, unless I knew, I'd not have guessed
the crows' feet on her face
were paint, nor that the grey came from a bottle.
It looked so natural.

At waist and wrist, her bones were blurred with fat
slapped on like clay.
How did she do it? I saw her, quite lately,
walking as slim and straight
as any girl her age. She had them fooled;
she looked for all the world

like one gone forty: only I knew better.
Just an odd thing
betrayed her; that way she had of eyeing
young men.... But then I knew her
so well. I couldn't see what others did,
and when I looked inside,

her eyes stared out, desperate and young.
I shook my head,
and she shook hers, and we almost collided.
I turned: she came along
beside me, mouthing: *It's me, I'm undercover.*
I wouldn't look at her.

Captain Roberts Goes Looting

It's best when they surrender. No time wasted
on violence: just a few swift kicks
to the officers' groins, for luck, and straight on
to serious matters.

An ox-roar: Valentine Ashplant's voice;
he's found the rum. Young Bunce is slashing bales
of silk to bright shreds. And the captain strolls
to the great cabin,

pauses at the door; breathes in the musk
and sandalwood: these hidalgos do themselves well,
and there's the china. White, fluted eggshell
you can see through;

he strokes it gently. *We had some of this
at Deseada: Val Ashplant smashed the last.*
(He's bellowing again: found the sugar
to make rum-punch.)

Will Symson eyes a woman passenger
and meditates rape. But the captain has found
the tea, twisted up in papers. He crushes
a leaf; sniffs. Lapsang,

smoky-scented, and the next is Oolong,
with its hint of peaches. Ashplant's delirious;
found the moidores that'll buy more sugar
and rum. Later,

back on their own sloop, the men cheer
the fire: they love watching a ship burn.
They've hauled over a hogshead of fine claret
to wash the deck;

it's like spilled blood, catching the fire's glint.
Captain Roberts sips peachy gold
from a translucent cup, wondering how long
it'll stay whole.

Captain Roberts Dresses for Battle

The gilt cheval glass has not been clean
since he took it from a French warship:
he peers through its clouds to the dull glow
of crimson damask. There's a long rip
in his breeches' arse, and an old gravy stain
on a sleeve whose lace cuff has gone yellow,
and he swears, softly, *ach y fi*: a long way
from Casnewydd Bach to the Bight of Biafra.

There was a sycamore outside our cottage,
I used to climb it.... What have I put
this sleeve in? He thinks back to when last
he stood before this glass: *was it the feast*
we gave that fort commander, Plunkett,
after he beat me in a swearing-match,
Welsh against Irish.... When we lay
off Sierra Leone; six weeks of venery,

oh the black velvet.... He slips a cross
of fine diamonds on, and for a second
the face that stares out of the fogged glass
is the governor of Martinique,
before they strung hemp round his neck
at the yard-arm.... *My folk lived inland:*
that tree was like a maintop, but I'd sway
on the high boughs, hoping to glimpse the sea.

Cabin, glass, image shudder: *grapeshot*
off the bow. How many crews have heard
my guns as close? The Sea King, the Fisher,
the Mercy, the Relief; small chance.... I've boarded
four hundred ships since I was a pirate,
and I'm thirty-nine. The man-of-war's fire
jars the glass again: a swift glint of gray
in his black hair. *This damn glass is filthy.*

Now the pistols, on their silk sling,
and the sword. *This is the last venture,*
one fight too many. And I will not go
to Corso, to hang a-sun-drying.
He bows to the glass, his red hat-feather
brushing its likeness on the plain of shadow.
Then out. And jumps on a gun-carriage, as lightly
as a boy on a branch, and turns the warship's way.

ID'S HOSPIT

I look out from a 17 bus:
more letters gone. ID'S HOSPIT
it says now, and one "I" hangs loose.
The stone front is like a film set,

nothing behind; no wards, just a waste patch.
Sunday car boot sales. No profit in land
right now, Danka; it doesn't pay them much
to build there yet.... A man turns half around,

looks at me oddly, and I know I spoke
aloud; spoke to you. I see you wave,
from the window where I would look back
after visiting, not wanting to leave

you and Richard. You'd be holding him,
a white parcel: *my son*. I felt unreal,
dizzy with light. Never such a time:
each night that week, the lads from the mill

took me out drinking. *Ryszard's got a boy*,
they'd tell the Taff Vale, the Panorama,
the Globe, the Greyhound and the red night sky;
a steel-town sky: you remember, Danka?

Not any more; years since I would see
a steel sunset. Jobs have got scarce
for the lads, and their lads. It's a harder city
than you knew, but there are places worse.

Under the high roads of Waterloo,
— you won't believe, Danka — people have put
a town of boxes up. I saw a soup queue.
Old times come round again: who would have thought?

And who thought they'd sell the corridors
where you walked singing? The things I miss:
pubs have dress codes and names like Traders,
and I talk to myself too much these days.

Our saint has lost his head, and the healing word
is flaking off the wall, letter by letter,
and I can't recall behind which board
was her window. I suppose it doesn't matter;

and perhaps tomorrow I will go to London,
back to the poor shacks in the concrete shadow,
and see if I cannot find my son
huddled in black, his face a boarded window.

Buffalo Bill's Triumphant Return to Pontcanna

He swept off his hat to the ladies, bowing low,
his white horse slow-pacing at the head
of hundreds, as the whole endless show
crossed Cardiff Bridge. Electric trams idled
behind, gleaming like the new century,
waiting for the Sioux nation to pass by.

In Sophia Gardens they set the tents up
as usual, and the gracious avenues
echoed with long-haired youths trying to war-whoop.
Shop-lads loitered; couldn't take their eyes
off the sullen boys their own age, who looked real
and belonged in books. Cody was critical

of the whoops: no spirit, you'd never think they were
their fathers' sons.... He bought Annie a macaroon
at Minifie's; she spun it high in the air
and shot it to crumbs. *This town sure has grown
since last time. There'll be twenty thousand tonight.*
Cody nodded: *Could be*, and thought about it,

about coal, iron, shipping, the Bute Docks
and the railroad, the way the goods go
to the great world. He thought of all the folks
who'd be paying their money down to see the shadow
of a dead time, not forty years away,
transmuted to story. *Oh girl, we've had our day,*

these guys are the future. He gave a great performance
that night; he still rode straight, and looked fine
in the right light, and from a fair distance,
but his heart was elsewhere. Who could ever imagine
a world dying so soon? He gazed out
over the amused faces: no fear of that

for them.... Their future's on tramlines, going forward
unswerving, founded on iron, anthracite-fuelled;
they'll never wake to find themselves outmoded,
showing curious strangers around their world....
Annie was shooting clays; her bright eyes narrowed
in their nest of feathery lines. He choked, and swallowed.

The Use of the Field

On the turn of the railway line after Taffs Well
lies a triangular field, a handkerchief.
It seems smoother, its green deeper, than most;
a Persian glow to it under the morning sun.
It is sheltered by cliffs, enclosed in a river's arm,
and it grows no crop. I have never seen it grazed
by sheep or cattle; no horses are pastured there.
Yet the grass is a lawn almost; close and gleaming,
— tended? For what? I look at the field, thinking,
always, *What is its use?* If not arable
nor pastureland; if nobody ever camps there,
if nobody rides trail bikes or flies kites?
What farmer, for a whim, grooms a field
and leaves it watching its face in the water,
its only witness, unless you count the windows
that mirror it a moment in passing?

The Flock

Far off across the valley, in a meadow,
a small white flock was grazing the steep slope.
Shadow chased sun, and sunlight followed shadow,
and they stayed still; none of them moved a step.

And then I looked again, and saw the church
watching its stony flock, who had no need
of shepherding; who could not feel the touch
of sun, nor the clouds' coldness overhead.

Insole Court: snow

Snow sifts down on the roof's grey forest;
caps the dead chimneys, dusts the pointed towers.
It is drifting high on the window-ledges,
but no sash is raised; no broom knocks

at the silence. Its soft weight snaps
the late roses; fills an old chain
of dry fishponds, slowly, like a dock
silting. Ships and coal built a house;

then the tide ebbed, and the hearths went dark,
and the sky empties so methodically.
The carved crevices of a lion's mane
whiten; smooth over, and he never stirs.

Steel-town Sunsets

"We used to have such sunsets", he said,
"you don't see them so bright anywhere
but a steel town. I loved the late shift;
orange, red, pink, spread out like a kid's painting
across the dark, and dust spinning
in all the lights..."
                              "That'd be pollution, right?"
I said it twice: no answer.
                              "Eh?"
"Pollution."
                    "Aye, I suppose." He stared out
at black towers against a grey dusk.

Outside

She's trying to see beyond her own image,
but it's dark outside, and the train window
is full of the lit carriage; passengers
reading, reflecting. She can't get past her face

to fields towns station names; her narrowed eyes
mock themselves. She's fretting over nothing,
she knows; nothing out there that matters,
but she can't help it; she feels as if

she's missing something, and the calm faces
crowd in, unknowing, driving her mad,
because there's something important outside
in the dark, unbeknown, past her face, slipping by.

Shore Lines

I. Redcoats

You know how it goes. The dark rockface
in the mist is a warship, a pirate brig,
but she stands off, taking the shore women
for soldiers in their cloaks of red flannel.

It was the French, or John Paul Jones;
it happened on every coast in Europe,
perhaps. Or maybe the shape hardened
after all into a ship; maybe the blurs
at the rail turned to grins, glinting eyes
that knew a woman when they saw one.

Those figures, stooped with seeding,
scrubbing, carrying; could they pass
for troopers? If they straightened,
kneading the ache from their backs;
if they shouldered their driftwood loads
like rifles; if they stood firm,
forcing themselves to look out
to where fear comes from?

Maybe it's even true that once
some young conscripts scrambled ashore
and surrendered to the first red cloak.
And she wide-eyed, watching a sea-wolf
turn up his scared boy's face.

II. The King of Sule Skerry

The woman with the black eye
limps under her creel to the tide's edge,
where wrack fetches up, salty and flyblown,
creaking underfoot. In freezing pools
she guddles for limpets to bait his line.
Out in the bay, a sleek head stands
proud of the water: shines at her.

"It is the king of Sule Skerry":
she drinks the calm in the wide eyes
like water. Her hands starve
for his streamlined flanks, his soft
spun whiskers; she aches to lay
her cheek to his cool pelt.

"Come ashore in a man's shape,
as you may do one night a year,
and I will hold you in a cave
and keep you from the cold white stars.

Then with the sun put on your skin,
and take me with you on the sea,
and show me where you reign the king
of all the selkies on Sule Skerry."

He balances easy; she cannot swim.
"Would you wait for me?"
She has seen them beached, wounded,
flinching from the fishermen.
One held her eyes in a dark look
of hopeless complicity, as the club
came down. They cry real tears.

"He says you tore his salmon-nets;
he made a fist of his red hand.
Away now, dark-eyes; don't wait.
My man will kill you, if he can."

III. The Monkey

It was not just Hartlepool,
oh no: I have come ashore
at so many ports, swung over
so many rails to stroll down
another quay.

I was always wearing
the jacket and the little cap
my shipmates sewed me; always
smiling up at new folk.
And always

they'd peer down, eyes narrowing,
faces clouding over. I always
chattered reassuringly, forgetting
they would take it for French.
You shore folk

are not like sailors at all.
So closed; so edgy. Soon
the whispered questions would start:
"Is it a Frenchman?"
"I wouldn't know:

what do they look like?"
"He might be; they're little,
the mounseers." "That's foreign,
that jabber of his." "Better
be safe than sorry."

And there I'd hang again
for a spy, a threat, a stranger,
an outlandish tongue. Where I went ashore,
it always seemed to be wartime,
and folk were always on edge.

Jeopardy

FOUR HUNDRED JOBS IN JEOPARDY —
it had to be worth
taking a look. But often,
along the road, he was tempted to stop.

Across Cloudcuckooland, it was free sex
all the way; in Cockaigne
roast pigeons flew obligingly
into his mouth. He could have lain
all day by the lemonade springs
of the Rock Candy Mountain.

But he knew where he had to go.
Oh, the gingerbread houses
were fun, and earning a wage
for sleeping late, and winning
races by coming last. But he knew
Jeopardy was still the place.

And it was; it was better
than all of them. At the border,
gates stood open; guards in deckchairs
glanced up to wave the refugees through.
A gleaming bus whizzed them
into the city, along wide avenues
shaded with plane trees, past parks
and playgrounds. He wandered clean streets,
shaking his head, gazing up
in awe at the crystal windows
of the great libraries. He breathed air
with no aftertaste, enrolled
in an evening class; found himself
a National Health dentist.

All night he lay awake,
wide-eyed, knowing he'd travelled,
at last, out of the world.

The Woodcarver of Stendal

"Judas? You want *Judas*? Look,
nobody wants Judas." But the bishop's clerk
was business-like, unbudging: "We've paid
for a full set of apostles, lad,
and we're 'avin' twelve."

Oh right, no trouble.... The worst man of all time.
I stare at the harmless wood, trying to see him,
the abhorred face. How do you carve evil?
I knew I'd need more than one model
to do him from life.

Anger: veins throbbing on the thick neck
of Master Klaus, who didn't like my work.
The glint of coin in miller Martin's face
as he gives wrong weight: old Liesl, drunk
                and shameless,
tugging your sleeve,

offering her blotched body.... Oh, my neighbours
were a great help, donating their coarse features
to my patchwork. I took the blemishes
of my kind, the worst in all of us,
to bring him alive.

But what happened then? He looks no sourer
than laughing Liesl; as honest as my old master,
who never paid me short; as sober a man
as Martin, who has eyes for no woman
but his plain wife.

Only a great sadness marks him out,
and that was mine. I scraped my heart
when I planed him. John, James, even Thomas,
they were names, nothing beside this Judas
noosed in my grief.

Frost Greyface

"General Frost on patrol
goes the rounds of his territory"
Nekrasov — *"Frost Rednose"*

This one does not come like a general,
bluff and booming, his tread shaking the night.
He sidles down the streets of the capital
soft-shod, soft-spoken, wearing a grey suit.

His hair is grey, and his expressionless face,
and greyness streams out of his fingers' ends,
silvering pavement cracks; misting the glass,
and silence grows, where he goes his rounds.

Frost Greyface is a fastidious fellow,
a conjuror: he likes to magic over
what's awkward and unsightly. Look now:
watch how he touches the huddle over there

in the doorway, and leaves it shimmering.
He hangs lace curtains to the cardboard shacks,
while on the black bin-bags, harshly wheezing,
you'd swear a thousand snails had left their tracks.

"Are you warm, lady?" Frost Greyface whispers
to an old woman about forty-one,
and she nods, and a sleepy smile wanders
on her blue lips, and she settles down

to stiffen like a white leaf on the tree.
Even the small smoke of her breath
on the air is unthreaded; she is nobody.
Frost Greyface laughs; leaps over her death

to make cobwebs glisten in the sun.
Now all the night's litter is swept away,
and the city flashes like new-minted coin,
fit to dazzle the very eye of day.

44

The Frozen

Tackling that peak, the whisper says,
you may come across an Austrian woman
frozen upright, swaying slightly, her face
empty as the luminous snow plain,
a sky bleached of blue in her eyes.

She stands sentinel, but many sleep
where they lay down, starved in the bright air.
White contours shift, and they turn up,
briefly, like folk who look round the door,
wave an apology and can't stop.

And they say ships endlessly circle
where the Arctic drift-ice snapped shut.
They have been seen, the crews that cannot fall
to rest, locked into their last minute.
There must be a legion of these people:

brittle chrysalids, rustling hollow
wherever light distils and breath comes hard,
seeing over the edge and mouthing *no*,
rueful signposts on the one road
nobody ever yet wanted to go.

Fellow-Feeling

He was South Efrican, with that eccent
you can't mistake:
he sold cigarettes to the Third World,
and his talk

was all markets, profits, gross.
He had no problem
with lung cancer; he said politics
wasn't for him,

though he did think of emigrating
"if power were to get
into the wrong hends". I couldn't take to
a man like that;

we'd nothing in common, except happening
to sit so close
at the snooker. Until the young player
passed next to us,

and my guts twisted with wanting
to stroke his hair,
and run my fingers along his spine's curve,
and I saw my neighbour,

white-knuckled, hungry eyes aching,
fixed on the remote
beautiful face, and I nearly said:
"hey, you too, mate?"

Teen Curfew in New Orleans

Dear city fathers of New Orleans,
won't the old town be a little *dull* at night
when you've swept all the sweet sixteens
off the streets? All the fragile girls, bright
as windsurfer sails; all the pale sexy boys?
So they're a menace, sometimes. It's called beauty:
it's irrational, disorderly, dangerous;
it's worth it. If I'm stuck with being forty,
at least I can still look at them. When you've turned
the cradle of jazz into Mogadon City,
just let me know. I won't be coming round.
I'll take my chances with the young and pretty,
and if I do get mugged, with my last breath
I'll thank them for not boring me to death.

The Embarkation of the Pigs

On hearing that British publishers no longer
welcome pig characters in children's books.

Piglet can take a hint. He walks off
page four, leaving a small white space
among the swirling snowflakes. Pooh wanders on,
his paw grasping at air, toward the place

where the Hundred Acre merges into Nutwood,
and Rupert stares at a Podgy-shaped gap.
Meanwhile, houses of brick, sticks and straw
open their doors, and out the Three step,

suitcases in their trotters. At every turn,
some other joins the band: on some page
a word fades. They follow Pigling Bland
down to the pea-green boat at the tide's edge,

that will take them to the eternal wood
where the Piggywig stands; where the round moon
will countenance their portly, tolerant curves.
This is where outlaws dance. Shine on; shine on.

Snowman

We built him; he was standing here.
I never saw him go away.
He was the first one of the year.

We went to Grandpa's for the day.
The sun was shining bright and clear.
When we came home, I ran to play,

and he was gone. He'd left his gear,
his hat and scarf and pipe of clay,
piled neatly on the grass, just here,

and no-one saw him go away.
I asked what made him disappear.
The silly things some people say:

"We couldn't have him always near.
Perhaps he had grown tired of play,
like our old cat that died last year."

Our cat would snooze most of the day,
but if I scratched behind his ear,
he'd smile and purr, as if to say:

"I still enjoy just being here."
I never saw him go away.
I picked up all the snowman's gear.

— The silly things some people say —
I thought that I could feel him near.
I know he would have liked to stay.
I never saw him go away.

Territories

This used to be her child-free room,
the zone the books tell you to keep
clear of their clutter. "Do be firm;
adults need somewhere to escape."
It never works, not at the time.

The toys were catapulted back,
or infiltrated, day by day.
Feeling besieged, she'd sometimes make
a sortie: sweep it all away,
then stand by for the next attack.

Then, suddenly, they seemed to raise
the siege. Behind their bedroom doors
they founded new territories.
She listens, sometimes, on the stairs,
to their Nintendo, their CDs,

or conversations just too low
to catch. She reads: ADULTS KEEP OUT
on the door; looks for things to do
about the house, rather than sit
in the retreat where they don't go.

Bumblebees and the Scientific Method

A scientist, a man of parts,
(some of which worked, in fits and starts),
by using certain apparatus
proved bees could not be aviators.
There was no doubt, declared our hero,
the fundamental laws of aero-
nautics, -dynamics and whatever
must soon convince the unbeliever
that bees were built to such a model,
they scarcely could do more than waddle.
The ratio of their body weight
to wing-span, he could demonstrate,
precluded take-off, much less flight.
Colleagues allowed his sums were right:
Professors, Fellows, Doctors, Tutors,
sweating away at their computers,
confirmed our man's results *in toto*,
and grudgingly agreed to go to
honour his triumph at a party,
(nobody really loves a smarty).
While all acclaimed his theories,
nobody thought to tell the bees,
who, never having been to college,
nor stayed abreast of modern knowledge,
kept up a stunning imitation
of wing-powered aerial navigation.

Booklifting

I slipped a Jean Genet inside my shirt
(he'd have approved, surely?) and sidled out,
a bit shiftily. Nothing went amiss,
so next day I half-inched a Martin Amis,
(come on, don't tell me *he* needs the dough?)
I palmed *The Communist Manifesto*
on the way, murmuring "Property is theft".
They'd no copies of *Trainspotting* left,
but they come in next week, and then I'll have it.
Sorry, Irvine, I've got a book habit
to feed; the library offers Mills & Boon,
but I need the real thing, not methadone,
and I'm broke. "Books were *meant* for the likes of us",
I said, as I found Salman a safe house.

Ciphers

The tides erode a wader's precise prints
to a smudge, and the snail's silver signature
dries faint. So words keep the shape
of thought, of that vastness which absorbs
definition as easily as a blue sky
sucks up the calligraphy of smoke.

TRANSLATIONS

DER WILDE ALEXANDER (13th Century)

Hie vor dô wir kinder waren
(Long ago when we were young...)

There was a time, oh, years back,
when we were children, and we'd take
our pleasure in the meadows,
here and there, as we chose.
There, where we'd find, now and then,
a violet hidden,
you can see cows grazing now.

I remember us sitting
among the flowers, arguing
about which was prettier.
That's how naive we were,
plaiting wreaths, dancing
in a childish ring.
And so time passes, my dear.

Look, that's where we used to search
for berries, between pine and birch,
over stock and over stone,
as long as the sun shone.
Then we'd hear through the bushes
the forester's cries:
"Children, go home now; go on."

Oh, the rashes we'd come out in,
picking berries, way back when,
yesterday.... It was great sport.
Sometimes we'd hear a shout
of warning from a herdsman:
"Take care, children,
there's a lot of snakes about."

A child wanders in the long grass;
suddenly he starts and cries:
"A snake just slithered by,
and it's bitten our pony,
and he'll never get well.
Go to hell
you lousy snake, with my curse!"

"Come, get out of the forest,
children! If you don't make haste
to leave the wood behind
while there's still light enough to find
your path, you'll go astray,
and all your play
will turn to tears, in the end.

There were five virgins, did you know,
who stayed so long in the meadow,
that the King barred his hall.
Well might they mourn and wail.
Every stitch they wore,
the guards tore,
and left them nothing at all."

ANDREAS GRYPHIUS (1616-1664)

Es ist alles Eitel
(All is vanity)

Nothing but vanity, look where you may.
What one man builds, another soon knocks down.
Here'll be a meadow, where was once a town,
and no-one but a shepherd boy at play.
Enjoy those flowers: they won't last the day,
and they who talk so high will soon be bone
and ash. What lasts; what metal or what stone?
When fortune smiles, a storm is on the way.
The fame of great deeds passes like a dream,
and how should man, time's shuttlecock, stand firm?
Most prized are dust and shadows in our eyes,
and wind, and void, and a flower we once found
in the field.... We search every inch of ground,
and miss the only thing that never dies.

Tränen des Vaterlandes: Anno 1636
(His country's tears: 1636)

How did we come so overwhelmed with war?
The wild, bold robber-bands, the bloodsoaked blade,
the screaming bugle, thundering cannonade,
have eaten all our labour, all our store.
The tower's afire; the church can stand no more,
the town hall's down, strong men lie maimed and dead,
young girls are forced: our eyes are daily fed
on flame, plague, death, that hurt to the heart's core.
Here in our town the river runs with blood:
three times six years have passed, since first it stood
so still, choked with the bodies of mankind.
Yet I say nothing of a loss more dire
than death; harder than hunger, plague or fire:
the precious souls despoiled, gone with the wind.

An Eugenien
(To Eugenia)

Rose of ladies, did you really not know
that time's pastime, this rose beyond compare,
could droop and fall, even as you held it here?
Eugenia, that's how we all go.
Why, time will scythe your body down just so.
Then eyes, brow, breast, will all go we know where,
shovelled into the musty ground, my dear,
where soon they'll sicken him who loves you now.
Nothing that lives, however bright it be,
can keep its colour or its constancy.
We have been death's elected from the start.
Nothing so rare, to measure with the rose,
whose opening brings her brief life to a close.
That's how it is with us: death at the heart.

Über die Erdkugel
(On the terrestrial globe)

This earth, this sphere that houses beasts and men,
is measured out, though none has seen it all.
Where feet have never trod, a mind can rule,
setting the bounds to lands and seas unseen.

Über die Himmelskugel
(On the celestial globe)

See the sky's likeness, figured by a man
sitting on earth! Why, what a mind is this,
that searches far beyond the reach of eyes,
creating heaven, as fits the heaven-born.

CHRISTIAN HOFMANN VON HOFMANNSWALDAU 1617-1679

Verliebte Arie
(Love Air)

Where did they wander,
those easy days
of my soul's first surrender,
when first I knew your face
was my commander?
All gone like smoke: it's true what people say,
that all desire must have its day.

The harmless flirting
that chained me so,
before I knew it, rooting
as deep as it would go,
now leaves me hurting.
You make it plain enough: I see quite well
that love's no anchor after all.

Sweet recollection
of pleasures past
will drive me to distraction.
Whatever cannot last
ends in affliction.
What once we taste, and must not taste again,
is void of joy; a dish of pain.

An amber savour,
a given kiss
will not stay sweet for ever;
their flavour fades and dies.
A dried-up river
cannot refresh. Nothing that pleases us
can spring from any time but this.

There was an ocean,
a skin of silk,
a life all exaltation.
And now I walk in black:
sad alteration.
Now may I weep, that love and shining sun
should turn to grief, when they go down.

PAUL FLEMING 1609-1640

Zur Zeit Seiner Verstossung
(When he was rejected)

A merchant who has trusted all his freight
upon one ship, is risking recklessly,
for that one wreck leaves him in beggary.
He with one hope is in a sorry state.
Look at me now: I see I'm wise too late.
My ship is sunk, my freight is floating free.
Nothing is all the salvage left to me:
she goes to him and leaves me to my fate.
Unhappy that I am, my heart is torn,
my sense is senseless and my spirit dies.
My all is nothing: what next, I can't guess.
I could have spared most things, except for one,
the greatest loss I suffered: my own soul.
I lost her, and I lost myself as well.

FRIEDRICH VON LOGAU 1604-1655

Ein Krieges-Hund redet von sich selbst
(A soldier's dog testifies)

Dogs who guard the farmer's herd,
dogs who fret upon a lead,
dogs who hunt or draw a cart,
dogs who stay where they are put,
dogs who beg for table scraps,
dogs who lie in ladies' laps,
all these dogs, it's plain to see,
come of duller stock than me.
I can't be as they all are,
for I serve the dogs of war.
I am at the heroes' side
when they stage a livestock-raid.
Thieves and I are of a kind;
robbery is to my mind.
When we're quartered, I bring in
geese and hens to feed my men;
when we're moving, I can flush
skulking peasants from the bush.
When the dolts complain because
someone's commandeered their horse,
I can see them off so soon,
they don't know which way to run.
I can lay the country waste,
eating, spoiling, with the best.
I've no time for country folk;
officers are what I like:
in my own line, after all,
I'm a canine general.

Schlaf und Tod
(Sleep and Death)

Sleep and death make all alike;
millionaire and stony broke,
upper crust and working man,
rogue and honest citizen.

Der Mensch
(Man)

Nine months prepare him for

                    the day he first draws breath,

and not a moment's grace

            to come to terms with death.

KALLIMACHOS 310-240 BC

Epigram to Lysanias

Bestselling blockbusters bore me stiff:
the more men travel a road, the less I like it.
The choice of many is no choice of mine:
I don't use the street-corner drinking-fountain,
nor any common, popular thing.
Even as I own your beauty drives me crazy,
I hear the echo whisper: *easy, easy.*

Acknowledgements

Some of these poems have previously appeared in the following publications: *Acumen, BABEL* (Germany), *The Bridport Prize Anthology 1995, Epoch* (New York), *Burning the Bracken: Fifteen Years of Seren Poetry* (Seren), *Intimate Portraits* (Seren), *The New Shetlander, The New Welsh Review, On The Third Day* (Gomer), *The PHRAS Prize Anthology 1995, Planet, Poetry Review, Poetry Wales, Tandem, The Western Mail, The Yellow Crane.*

All the translations are from the German except for the final one from Kallimachos which is from the Greek.